How BIG was NOAH'S ARK?

and Other Questions Kids Ask About the Bible

Betsy Rosen Elliot

Illustrated by Don Page

INSPIRATIONAL PRESS

NEW YORK

Kurt Boyles

First Inspirational Press edition published in 1998.

Inspirational Press
A division of BBS Publishing Corporation
386 Park Avenue South
New York, NY 10016

Inspirational Press is a registered trademark of BBS Publishing Corporation.

Published by arrangement with RD Publishing Services.

Library of Congress Catalog Card Number: 98-72392

ISBN: 0-88486-221-6

Printed in Hong Kong.

 CONTENTS

How BIG Was Goliath?

Answers to kids' questions about the Old Testament

THAT'S BIG!

Who wrote the Bible?

Who wrote the Bible?
The Bible was written by different people whom God inspired. Some of these writers were great leaders like Moses and David. David was a shepherd who became a king!

What does _Bible_ mean?
The word _Bible_ comes from the Greek word _biblia_, which means _books_. The Bible is actually a collection of 66 books!

What is a prophet?

A prophet is someone who speaks for God. Sometimes a prophet tells us about the future. Isaiah wrote about the coming Messiah, God's special person. Other times a prophet tells the truth about right now. Nathan told David about the secret bad things God knew David was doing.

Why do we call the Old Testament *old*?

The Bible is made up of the Old and New Testaments. The whole book is old but when we talk about the Old Testament, we mean the old agreement between God and his people. When Jesus came, he gave us a new agreement: the New Testament.

Is Jesus in the Old Testament?

No...and yes! The Old Testament books don't name Jesus directly. But some books, like Isaiah and the Psalms, do tell us a lot about him. They call him the *Messiah*, or God's special person.

How did God make people?

How did God make people?

God made the first man, Adam, out of dust and breathed life into him. While Adam was sleeping, God took out one of his ribs and made it into the first woman, Eve.

GIRAF

WART-HOG

Where did Adam and Eve live?

Adam and Eve lived in a beautiful place called the Garden of Eden. There was a river flowing through it. Nobody knows exactly where Eden was, but many think it was in Iraq. There were many animals living in the Garden and God let Adam choose their names!

What did Adam and Eve do wrong?

Adam and Eve disobeyed God. God told them that they could eat from every tree in the Garden except one in the center of the garden. A serpent convinced Eve that God was just being mean. So Adam and Eve ate the forbidden fruit. Their special friendship with God was badly hurt.

Did Adam and Eve have many children?

Adam and Eve had three sons that we know a little about. Cain, the oldest, was a farmer. The next son, Abel, was a shepherd. Cain got angry because God liked Abel's offering instead of his, so he killed Abel. The third son was Seth and he lived to be 912 years old!

How big was Noah's ark?

How big was Noah's ark?
The ark was 137 metres long (longer than a football field), 23 metres wide (put five cars end to end) and 14 metres tall (like a very big house)!

Did other people go into the ark with Noah?
Noah's wife and his three sons, Shem, Ham, and Japheth went. His three sons each took their wives as well. That made eight people in the ark.

How many animals went into the ark?
Noah took two or more of every kind of bird and animal that you can imagine; plus a few more! Nobody knows the exact number of animals in total, but it must have been a pretty noisy ark!

How long did it take Noah to build the ark?

It probably took Noah about 120 years to build the ark! And Noah was about 480 years old when God told him to start building! He was 950 years old when he died.

WHEW!!!

Why did God make a flood?

People were doing bad things. They cheated and hurt each other. They didn't worship God. And they didn't care for the earth. God was sad he had ever made people and he decided to start over.

ARE WE THERE YET?

When did the first rainbow appear?

God sent the first rainbow after the flood. It was a sign of his promise to Noah that he would never again flood the whole earth. So whenever you see a rainbow, you know that however much it rains, God has promised he won't let it rain so much that it will flood the whole earth!

What was so amazing about Joseph's coat?

What was so amazing about Joseph's coat?
Joseph's coat had many colors. Clothes in those days were not colorful like they are today so it would really have stood out! But the coat was special because his father, Jacob, gave it to him. It showed how much his father loved him.

Why were his brothers jealous?
Joseph was Jacob's favorite son and Jacob's other sons were jealous. They also hated Joseph's dreams about how he would one day be the boss. They were so upset they threw him in a pit and sold him as a slave to Egypt.

Why were dreams special to Joseph?
Joseph's dreams were messages from God about the future. In Egypt, God told him that Pharaoh's dreams about cows and grain were a warning about a famine, or shortage of food, to come.

What did Joseph do in Egypt?

Potiphar bought Joseph as a slave but soon put him in charge of his household. Potiphar's wife lied about Joseph and he was unfairly put in prison. But he was freed so he could explain Pharaoh's dream. Pharaoh was so impressed, he put Joseph in charge of everything in Egypt!

Did he ever see his brothers again?

There was a famine everywhere. But in Egypt, Joseph had stored plenty of food ahead of time. Egypt sold food to other countries. So Jacob sent his sons to Egypt to buy grain. Joseph told them who he was and the family came together again. Jacob, his sons and their families moved to Egypt.

Can a bush really talk?

Can a bush really talk?
Bushes can't talk unless God chooses to make them! He did with Moses. Moses saw a bush on fire, yet it didn't burn up! The bush started calling his name. It was really God who used the bush to get Moses' attention. God wanted Moses to know that his people would soon be free.

Why was baby Moses in the bulrushes?
God's people were slaves in Egypt, and Pharaoh ordered all their boy babies to be killed. He was afraid they would grow up to fight him. So Moses' mother hid him in a basket and floated it on the Nile River by the bulrushes, or reeds. When Pharaoh's daughter came to bathe at the river she found Moses. Moses' name means *taken out of the water*.

What was *manna*?
The first time God's people saw this stuff on the ground they asked, *manna*? In Hebrew this means, *what is it?* God's people wandered in the desert for 40 years before they reached the Promised Land. There weren't any shops so each morning God gave them white, breadlike stuff. It tasted like wafers made with honey. The name stuck and they called it *manna*.

Why didn't God's people just swim across the Red Sea?

Swimming would have been hard for the Israelites in regular clothes and when they were carrying things! Instead, God helped them escape from the Egyptians by making a great wind push the water back to make a path to the other side. But when the Egyptians tried to cross, the water came back and drowned them. God chose to do a special miracle to save his people so that their faith would grow.

Special people and animals

Are there any famous children in the Bible?
Joash was only seven years old when he was crowned king! Esther has a whole book written about her. She was an orphan and a Hebrew slave who became a queen of Persia! Samuel was only a boy when God first called him to become a prophet.

Are there any famous animals in the Bible?
The lion is the animal mentioned most in the Bible. Sheep appear often. The eagle was considered special because of its strength and speed. When Elijah hid in the desert, ravens brought him food every day. Once, Balaam's donkey talked and tried to warn him about an angel in the road!

How did David, a shepherd, become a king?
When Saul stopped being a good king, God sent the prophet Samuel to David's family. David's seven brothers seemed more like kings than David, the youngest. But God told Samuel that the young shepherd really loved God. Then Samuel poured oil on his head, and David went to serve Saul. David became king after Saul died.

How did Joshua win the battle of Jericho?

God told Joshua to trust him and to have all the people march around the city of Jericho once a day for six days. Then on the seventh day, they were to march around the city seven times while the priests blew trumpets. The people obeyed God, and then shouted loudly, and the walls of Jericho tumbled down!

Why was Daniel thrown to the lions?

Why was Daniel thrown to the lions?
Daniel was being punished because he wouldn't stop praying to God. Darius, King of Babylon, had been tricked into making a law against people praying to anyone but him. Darius tried to keep Daniel from the lions, but he was forced to follow his own law when Daniel kept on praying.

Why didn't the lions eat him?
Daniel was unhurt because God protected him. God sent an angel to shut the lions' mouths. King Darius was so amazed that he made a new law: everyone in his kingdom had to worship Daniel's God!

Why was Daniel in Babylon?

Daniel was captured and taken prisoner. He was probably a teenager when he was taken to Babylon. He was from one of the royal families of Judah and was handsome and smart. King Nebuchadnezzar trained Daniel for three years before Daniel could serve him. Daniel was about 70 when he was thrown to the lions.

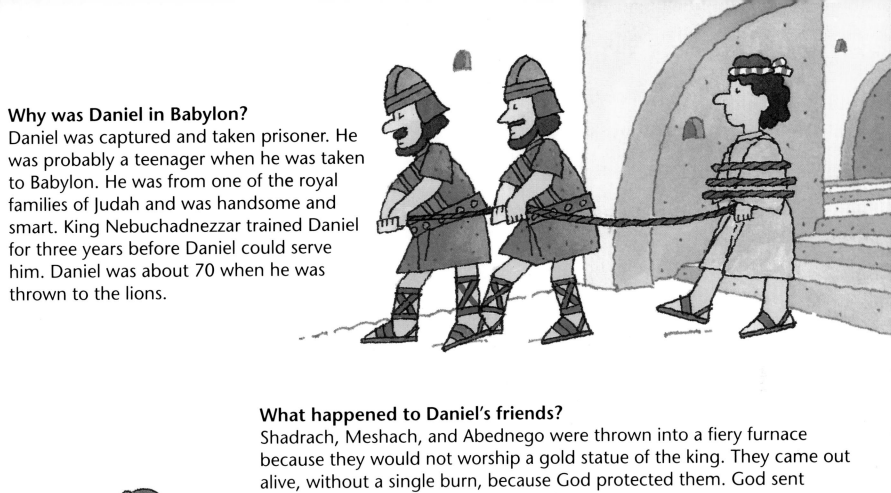

What happened to Daniel's friends?

Shadrach, Meshach, and Abednego were thrown into a fiery furnace because they would not worship a gold statue of the king. They came out alive, without a single burn, because God protected them. God sent someone special to walk in the flames with them.

How big was the big fish?

How big was the big fish?
The big fish that God sent to swallow Jonah might have been a whale. It was large enough for Jonah to live inside for three days and nights!

Why was Jonah running away?
God had a job for Jonah. He was to go to Nineveh, the capital of the enemy nation, Assyria. God wanted Jonah to tell the people to follow God, but Jonah ran away. He didn't want to help his enemies.

What happened to Jonah?
Jonah got on a ship. Then God made a terrible storm and the ship was about to sink. Jonah knew that the storm was his fault because he was running away from God. He begged to be thrown overboard. Immediately the storm stopped. Then God sent a big fish to save Jonah.

Why didn't Jonah suffocate inside the fish?
God wasn't finished with him yet. Jonah prayed from inside the fish, thanking God for saving him. God then told the fish to spit Jonah onto dry land.

Did people listen to Jonah after he got out of the fish?
Jonah went to Nineveh and told them, "Forty more days and Nineveh will be destroyed." The people listened and were sorry. When God saw how they changed, the city was spared.

Record breakers!

How strong was Samson?
Very strong! One day he defeated a lion with his bare hands. Soon after, he fought 30 men at one time and won! Another time, he defeated 1,000 men with a donkey's jawbone. Samson was so strong, he was able to push the pillars of a temple so that it came crashing down.

Who was the smartest person in the Bible?
King Solomon was the most famous for his wisdom. When he became king of Israel, God asked him what he would like for a gift. Instead of asking for riches, Solomon asked for an *understanding heart* and a mind to know right and wrong. God gave him what he wanted. We can see his wisdom in the book of Proverbs, for example.

HE'S SMART!

How big was Goliath?
The Philistine giant was over nine feet tall. His helmet and his armor were made of bronze. The huge spear that he carried had a 25-pound spearhead.

THAT'S BIG!

Who was the oldest person in the Bible?
Many people in the Bible lived to be much older than people do today. Methuselah, who was Noah's grandfather, was 969 years old when he died!

Who was the youngest king in the Bible?
Joash was seven years old when he became king. He was faithful to God, but he didn't make any real changes to help people follow God.

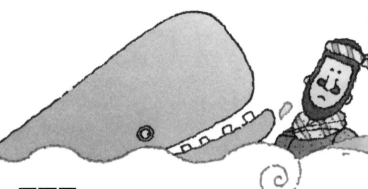

Did Jesus Wear Blue Jeans?

Answers to kids' questions about the New Testament

What is a Gospel?

What is a Gospel?

Gospel means *good news* in Greek. The Gospels are the first four books of the New Testament. They tell about Jesus and how he came to earth to show us God's love by his life, death and rising to life again. He gave us a new start with God. That's certainly good news!

Why do we have four Gospels?

The four Gospels were written for four different reasons. Matthew wrote his Gospel for Jewish people. Mark wrote his to give the basic facts (it is the shortest). Luke wrote his Gospel to give all the details of Jesus' life. John wrote his Gospel to show that Jesus is our Savior, or rescuer.

Who wrote the New Testament?

There are 27 books in the New Testament and many people wrote them! Jesus' friends wrote some. Paul, who once hated Christians and later became a Christian himself, wrote many others. Luke was a doctor and he wrote a Gospel and the book of Acts.

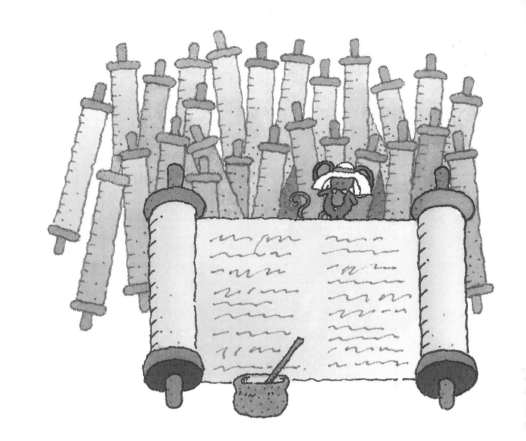

YOUR MAIL, MADAM.

Are the New Testament letters like the ones we write today?

Yes, except they weren't written on paper and envelopes and mailed. They were usually written on rolled-up scrolls made of parchment, and they were carried by messengers or travelers. Some of the letters were written to one person, but most were sent to churches and read to everyone.

Why was Jesus born in a stable?

Why was Jesus born in a stable?
All the inns in Bethlehem were full and Mary and Joseph needed a place to stay. Since there were no rooms, Mary and Joseph stayed in a stable and that's where Jesus was born. Jesus actually slept in a manger. A manger is the box that holds clean hay for the animals.

Why did the three wise men bring such strange gifts?
God was showing the three wise men who Jesus would grow up to be. Gold showed Jesus would become a king. Frankincense showed that Jesus should be worshipped. Myrrh showed that Jesus' death was to be very important.

What was Jesus' last name?

Jesus didn't have a last name. People in Jesus' time were often given their name by where they lived, such as *Saul of Tarsus*, or by their fathers, like *James and John, sons of Zebedee*. When we say *Jesus Christ*, the word *Christ* isn't his last name. It means that Jesus was the Christ, or Savior. People also called him *Jesus of Nazareth*.

Was Jesus ever naughty?

Jesus was a person just like you and me, but he never, ever did anything wrong! His parents did get cross with him though. When he was 12 years old, he was traveling with his parents and they lost him. They were with a large group so they didn't realize at first that he was missing. They found him in the temple, asking and answering questions.

Did Jesus wear blue jeans?

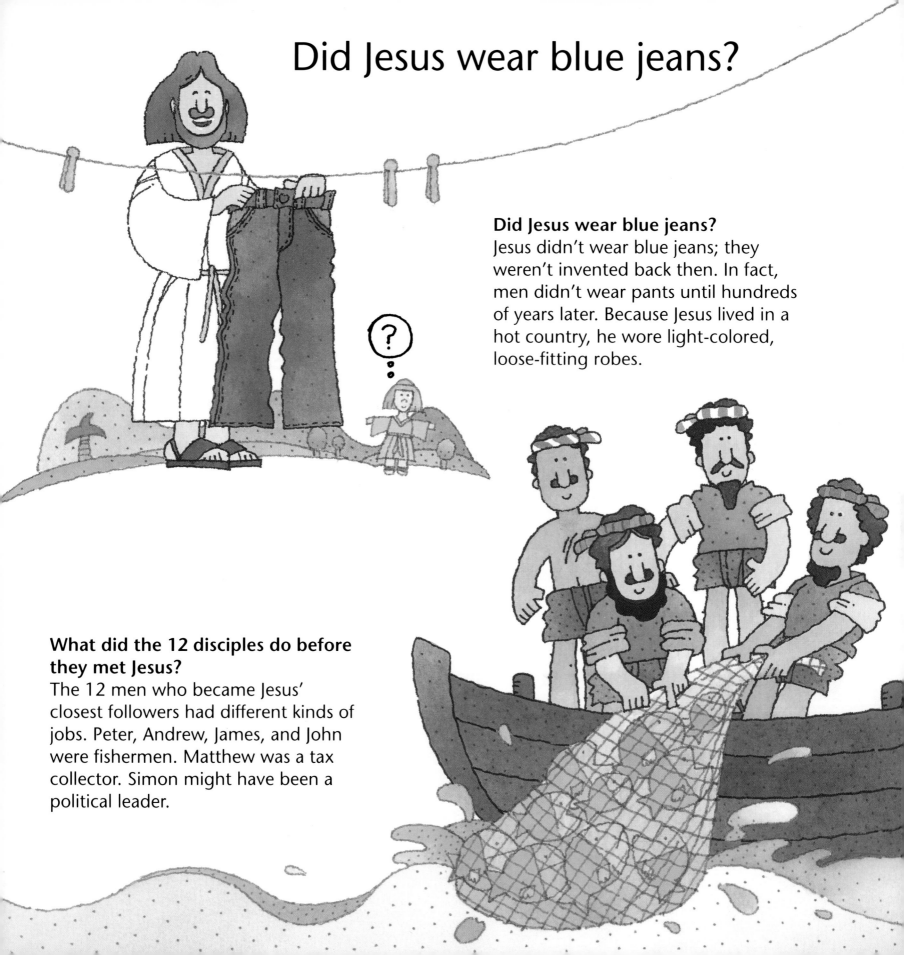

Did Jesus wear blue jeans?
Jesus didn't wear blue jeans; they weren't invented back then. In fact, men didn't wear pants until hundreds of years later. Because Jesus lived in a hot country, he wore light-colored, loose-fitting robes.

What did the 12 disciples do before they met Jesus?
The 12 men who became Jesus' closest followers had different kinds of jobs. Peter, Andrew, James, and John were fishermen. Matthew was a tax collector. Simon might have been a political leader.

Who were some of Jesus' closest friends?
Peter, James, and John seemed to be Jesus' closest friends. One day Jesus took them on a mountain top to show them what a special messenger of God he was. And as he died, Jesus told his mother and John to be like mother and son.

Why was Peter nicknamed *Rock*?
The name *Peter* in Greek is *Petros*. This means *rock*. So Jesus was saying that Peter could be as solid as a rock. Peter lived up to his nickname. He became a great leader in the early church.

Did Jesus know Moses?

Did Jesus know Moses?
No, Jesus didn't know Moses because Jesus was born more than 1,000 years later. But Jesus knew a lot about Moses. Also, Moses appeared with Jesus on a mountain top. This showed Jesus' friends how special Jesus was.

Why did the paralysed man go through the roof?
A man who couldn't walk had some clever friends. They couldn't get through the door of the house where Jesus was because of all the people. So they removed part of the roof! They lowered the man down on ropes so that Jesus could heal him!

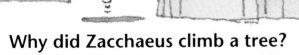

Why did Zacchaeus climb a tree?
Zacchaeus was a short man and he couldn't see Jesus over the crowd. So he climbed a tree to get a better view. Jesus noticed Zacchaeus and invited himself to Zacchaeus' house. Zacchaeus became a loyal follower of Jesus that day.

Who washed Jesus' feet?

Jesus was at a special dinner the week before he died. Mary, who was the sister of Lazarus and Martha, poured expensive perfume on Jesus' feet and gently washed them. Instead of using a towel, she dried Jesus' feet with her hair. Some people criticized Mary, but Jesus said she'd done a wonderful thing.

Did Jesus like children?

Children were special to Jesus. Once, Jesus' friends made some children go away. They thought the children were bothering Jesus. But Jesus told the children to stay; he said grown-ups could learn a lot from children!

What is a miracle?

What is a miracle?
A miracle is a wonderful thing that only God can do. Jesus did many miracles to help and heal people. It was a miracle when Jesus told the fierce storm to stop, and it did! These miracles proved that Jesus was God as well as man.

What was the first miracle Jesus did?
Jesus and his friends went to a wedding. Jesus' mother was there too. At the wedding party, the wine suddenly ran out. Jesus asked for some big jars to be filled with water and he turned the water into wine!

What other miracles did Jesus do?

Jesus brought some dead people back to life. He healed many who couldn't walk. He put mud on a blind man's eyes to make him see! He touched a man's tongue to make him talk! Twice Jesus fed thousands of people with just a little bit of food.

Why did Jesus walk on water?

One night Jesus' friends set out in a boat. It was very windy, so they found it hard to row. Jesus walked out on top of the water to them, calming the wind and calming their fears. The disciples realized Jesus was God on earth.

Did Jesus tell jokes?

Did Jesus tell jokes?

Jesus enjoyed life, and he could see the funny side of things. He seemed to like word jokes a lot. Once he said some people avoid little sins but ignore big ones. He said it is like someone who strains out a tiny bug from their drinking water ... but doesn't notice the camel in it!

Who got a job feeding pigs?

Jesus told a story about a man who left home to spend his money on silly things. Soon his money ran out and he had to feed pigs. He went back home and told his father he was sorry. His father welcomed him and gave him a big hug. That's just like God welcomes us when we are sorry.

Why did Jesus say people were like sheep?

Jesus said people were like sheep because sheep are not the smartest animals! Sheep need protection from enemies such as wolves or bears. They need a shepherd to care for them. Like sheep, people can easily follow wrong ways too. That's why we can be glad that Jesus is our Good Shepherd.

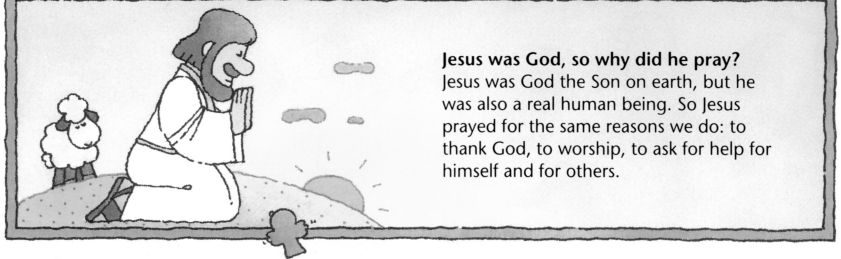

Jesus was God, so why did he pray?

Jesus was God the Son on earth, but he was also a real human being. So Jesus prayed for the same reasons we do: to thank God, to worship, to ask for help for himself and for others.

Why did Jesus ride a donkey?

Why did Jesus ride a donkey?

Jesus rode a gentle donkey into Jerusalem on Palm Sunday. He could have ridden a mighty war-horse, but he wanted to show that he was bringing peace and love.

What was the *last supper*?

The *last supper* was the last meal that Jesus and his disciples ate together. It was a Passover meal, a special supper to remember when the Israelites left Egypt. It was also special because it was the first Communion, a new way Jesus gave to remember him.

Why didn't Jesus defend himself?
Jesus was certainly powerful enough to fight back when he was arrested and nailed on the cross. But he knew that it was God's plan for him to die so that all people could have new life.

Why did Jesus wash his friends' feet?
When Jesus took a bowl of water and a towel and knelt to wash their feet, his friends were very surprised! This was the job of the least important servant, and Jesus was their master! Jesus wanted to show them he loved them and that they should serve one another.

Why did the sky turn dark?
When Jesus died, the sky turned dark for three hours. It was a sign from God that the most important event of history had happened.

Who rolled the stone away?

Who rolled the stone away?
Jesus was buried in a tomb like a cave with a huge stone in front to block the entrance. There were guards around the tomb to stop anyone from stealing Jesus' body. Matthew's Gospel says that an angel rolled the stone away.

Why did Jesus come back from the dead?
Jesus came back from the dead to prove he was more powerful even than death. He was God as well as a man, so death could not beat him. Jesus wanted to show his disciples (and us!) that he was worth believing in. He also had some work for them (and us!) to do here on earth; to share the good news.

Where is Jesus now?
Jesus is in Heaven now, preparing a place for us. He has given us his own spirit, the Holy Spirit, to help us each day.

What will happen when Jesus comes back?
The Bible tells us that a new Heaven and a new earth will begin when Jesus comes back to earth.

What was the first church like?

What was the first church like?
The first Christians didn't meet in church buildings. They met in homes because it was illegal and even dangerous to meet. But they met together for the same reasons we do: to worship God, to learn about Jesus, to pray, and to be with believers.

SHHH....

Were God's people always called Christians?
After Jesus died Christians were called *believers* or *followers of the Way*. Later the word *Christian* was used. It means *belonging to Christ*. When it was dangerous to be known as a Christian, Christians had a secret sign. The secret sign of a Christian was the sign of the fish.

What happened to the 12 disciples?

Some of the disciples, like Peter and John, became important leaders in the church. Some were killed for believing in Jesus. Some wrote books in the New Testament. John was busy: he wrote a Gospel, three letters and the book of Revelation!

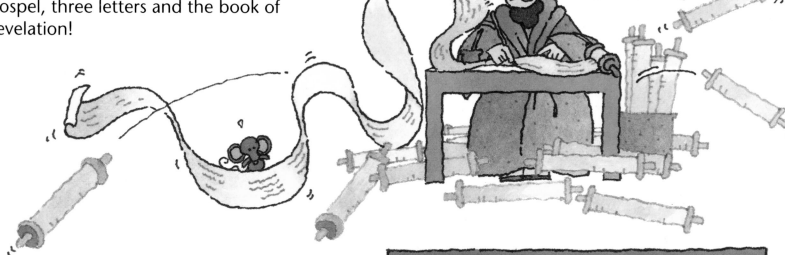

Where did Paul go on his travels?

Paul travelled in Europe, especially in Greece, and in Asia sharing the good news of Jesus. He travelled by boat and over land and he even got shipwrecked. On different trips Barnabas, John Mark and Luke went with him.

Why was Paul in prison?

Paul was put in prison at least five times! He was being punished for telling the good news about Jesus. Some people were afraid of the power of this message. They thought that by stopping the messenger, they could stop the message. But they were wrong! Churches just kept growing and the good news just kept spreading.